SYMBOLS OF AMERICA

Pat Daniel Jones

BeaLu Books

Copyright © 2020 by Pat Daniel Jones

All rights reserved. No part of this publication may be reproduced in any form or by any electronic or mechanical means, including information storage and retrieval systems, without the express written permission from the publisher, except in the case of brief quotations embodied in critical articles or reviews. For information regarding permission, contact BeaLu Books.

ISBN Hardcover: 978-1-7341065-4-1
ISBN Paperback: 978-1-7333092-7-1

Library of Congress Control Number: 2019952466
Publisher's Cataloging-in-Publication Data is on file with the publisher.

Edited by: Luana K. Mitten
Book cover and interior design by Tara Raymo • creativelytara.com

Printed in the United States of America
October 2019

BeaLu Books
Tampa, Florida

www.BeaLuBooks.com

PHOTO CREDITS: Cover: © wenani, © rokopix, © Andrea Izzotti, © skreidxeleu; Page 1: © rozbyshaka, Page 3: © Ranier Lesniewski, © Gianna Stadelmyer, © wavebreakmedia; Page4: © YuniqueB; Page 5: © Cgrealms; Page 6: © Andrea Izzotti; Page 7: © amadeustx; Page 8: © skreidzelev; Page 9: © NPS; Page 10: © Lone Wolf Photography; Page 11: rokopix; Page 12-13: © US Diplomacy Center; Page 14: © fluke samed, © Denise Torres, © rsooll; Page 15: © GoodAndy45; Page 16: © Matt Antonino; Page 17: Monkey Business Images, ESB Professional

"Oh, say can you see" the American symbols all around you?

A symbol is an object that represents something else. Symbols remind us of important concepts. Let's see if you know what these American symbols are and what they stand for.

DO YOU RECOGNIZE THIS SYMBOL?

Each color of the flag has a special meaning.

Red represents bravery.

White stands for purity and innocence.

Blue symbolizes justice.

Did you know the flag has nicknames? If you hear someone say "Old Glory" or "The Stars and Stripes," you'll know they are referring to the American Flag.

This is the flag of the United States of America. It has thirteen stripes with a red stripe at the top and the bottom. The stripes stand for the thirteen original colonies that declared their independence from England. Can you name the thirteen colonies?

In the top, left corner of our flag is a field of blue with fifty white stars. There are fifty states in the United States. Each star represents a state. Which state do you live in? How many states can you name?

Americans celebrate Flag Day on June 14. To show respect for the flag, many people put their right hand over their heart when they say *The Pledge of Allegiance* or when the National Anthem is played.

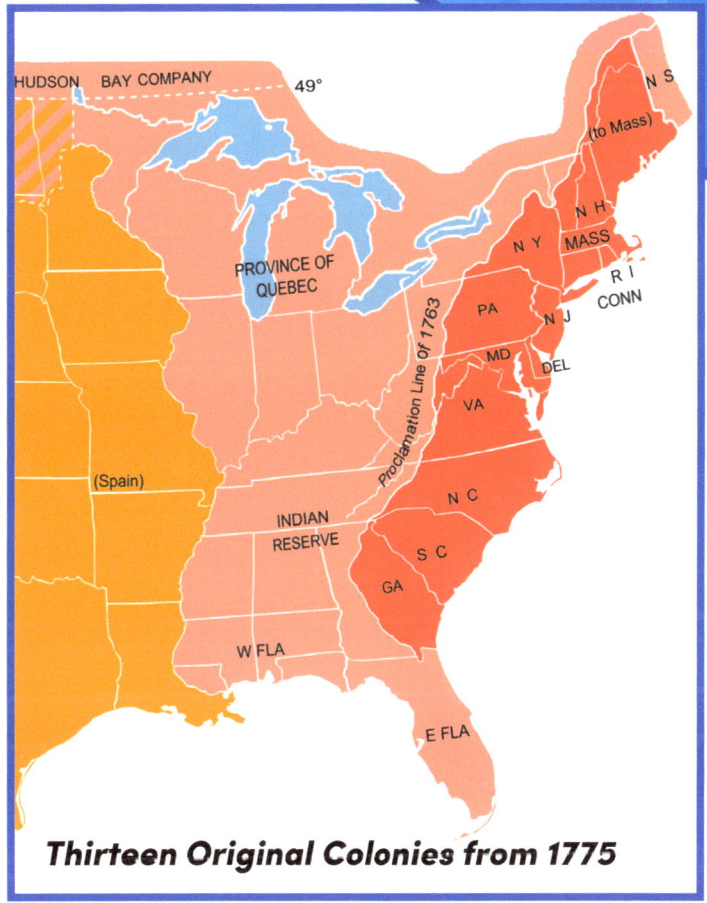

Thirteen Original Colonies from 1775

FUN FACT

The Star-Spangled Banner is the National Anthem of the United States. It was originally written in 1814 as a poem by Francis Scott Key. The poem's title was *The Defense of Fort McHenry*. I'm glad they changed the name when it was made the National Anthem.

DO YOU KNOW WHY A DIFFERENT FAMILY MOVES INTO THIS HOUSE EVERY FOUR OR EIGHT YEARS?

President Theodore Roosevelt officially named the President's House the White House in 1901. It is made of Aquia Creek sandstone and was painted with a lime-based whitewash which made it look white. Today it takes 570 gallons of paint to cover the outside.

It's because this house, known as the White House, is home to the President of the United States of America and his or her family. The White House is very large. In fact, it was the largest house in the United States until after the Civil War. It is about the size of thirty houses and covers 55,000 square feet.

The president's family lives in the center on the top two floors. George Washington, the first United States president, is the only president to live in a different house. The second president, John Adams, and his wife, Abigail, moved into the President's House on November 1, 1800. The president's office, called the Oval Office, is in in the West Wing of the White House.

The White House is the only private home of any country's leader that is open to visitors free of charge. About 6,000 people visit the White House every day. People come from all around the world to visit this American symbol.

FUN FACT

The White House has six floors. It sits on eighteen acres of land and has tennis courts, a putting green, a swimming pool, a movie theater, a bowling lane, a jogging track, and a lot more including:

★ 2 basements
★ 3 elevators
★ 3 kitchens
★ 28 fireplaces
★ 35 bathrooms
★ 132 rooms
★ 147 windows
★ 412 doors

DO YOU KNOW WHAT THIS SYMBOL IS?

The torch is a symbol of enlightenment.

The seven rays represent the seven continents in the world.

The table has the Roman numerals July IV, MDCCLXXVI etched on it to commemorate when the United States declared its independence from England.

The broken chain represents freedom from oppression and tyranny.

The Statue of Liberty is covered in 305 copper pieces. But today instead of looking like a copper penny, Lady Liberty looks green. A chemical process, called oxidation, is responsible for her color change.

This is the Statue of Liberty that stands on Liberty Island in New York Harbor. Lady Liberty welcomed millions of immigrants as they came to the United States through the Federal Immigration Station located on Liberty Island's neighbor, Ellis Island. Even now, the Statue of Liberty is a symbol of freedom and democracy throughout the world.

The people of France gave the statue to the United States. The 305 copper pieces were shipped in 214 crates. The pieces sat in a warehouse for a year while workers completed the statue's pedestal. President Grover Cleveland accepted the gift from France. It was dedicated on October 28, 1886 (after the Civil War).

Have you heard the words "...Give me your tired, your poor, Your huddled masses yearning to breathe free..." when people talk about the Statue of Liberty? The words are from a poem, *The New Colossus*, that was written by Emma Lazarus. She wrote the poem in November 1883 for an arts festival to help fund the Statue of Liberty's pedestal. Emma Lazarus died on November 19, 1887. A plaque with *The New Colossus* was added to Lady Liberty's pedestal in 1903.

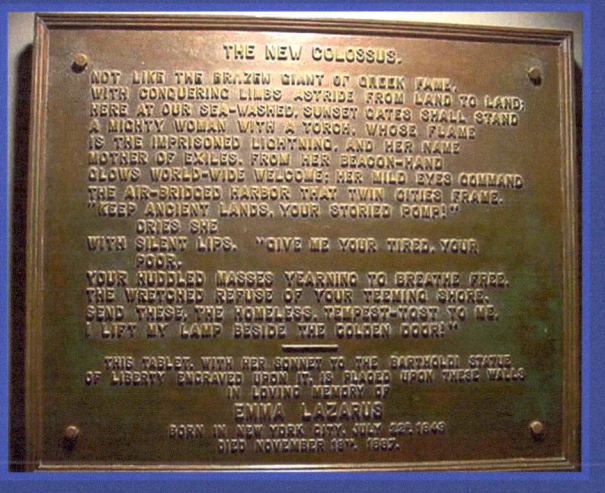

FUN FACT

The Statue of Liberty is big. It is taller than eight school buses lined up.

★ Height from ground to torch = 305 feet 6 inches
★ Height from base to torch = 151 feet 6 inches
★ Height of Face = 8 feet
★ Length of feet = 25 feet
★ Weight = 225 tons or 450,000 pounds
★ Number of stairs to reach the crown = 354
★ Number of windows in the crown = 25

DO YOU KNOW WHAT BIRD SYMBOLIZES THE UNITED STATES OF AMERICA?

Bald doesn't always mean no hair or feathers. It can also mean that an animal's head is marked with white.

It's the majestic bald eagle. The white feathers on its head represent truth and justice. Bald eagles are chief over all birds; flying higher than any other bird. Bald Eagles have large eyes that give them excellent vision. Their talons are strong and powerful so they can catch and carry fish and small animals. The bald eagle symbolizes freedom and power.

On June 20, 1782, the bald eagle was chosen to be the National Emblem of the United States. But June 20th wasn't named American Eagle Day until 1995 when President Bill Clinton proclaimed it.

FUN FACT

Eagles have amazing eyesight. Eagles have 5 times the number of light-sensitive cells in their retina as humans. Also, humans only see three basic colors (red, yellow, blue), but eagles see many more variations and UV colors. That's why eagles can distinguish camouflaged prey from a long distance.

★ Bald eagles reach speeds of 75-99 miles per hour in flight.
★ Bald eagles can glide as high as 10,000 feet in the sky.
★ A bald eagle's wingspan is longer than you are tall.
★ Females wingspan = 7 feet
★ Males wingspan = 6 feet

Now that you know how important the bald eagle is in representing the United States of America, you can understand why it is featured on the Great Seal of the United States. The eagle is holding a ribbon with the phrase *E Pluribus Unum* on it. This phrase was the original motto of the United States. It means "out of many, one," or just another way of saying the United States. Let's find out what the rest of the things on the front of the seal represent.

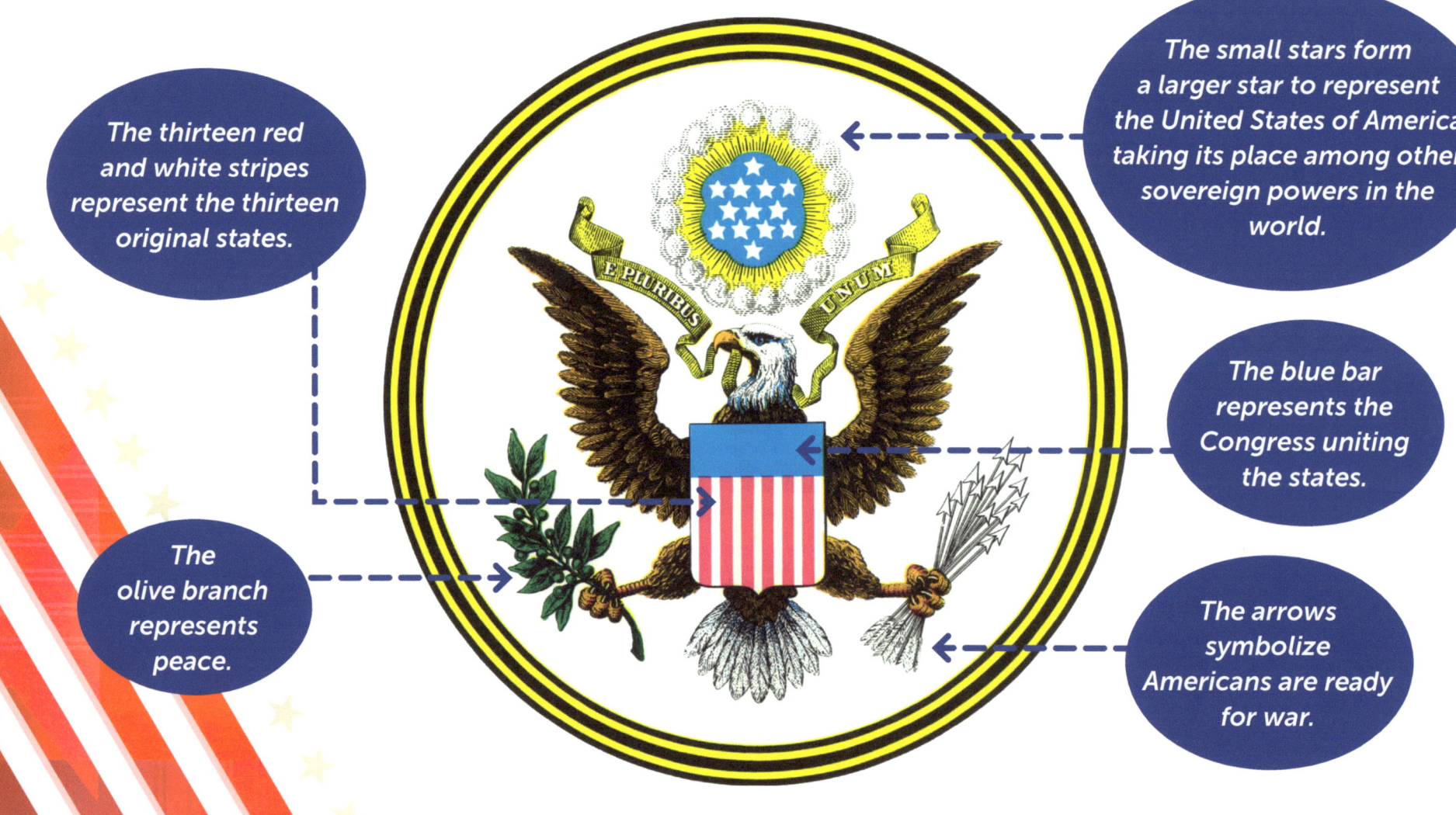

The thirteen red and white stripes represent the thirteen original states.

The small stars form a larger star to represent the United States of America taking its place among other sovereign powers in the world.

The olive branch represents peace.

The blue bar represents the Congress uniting the states.

The arrows symbolize Americans are ready for war.

The back side of the Great Seal of the United States features a thirteen-step pyramid in the center. This represents strength and duration.

The eye at the top of the pyramid with the words Annuit Coeptis means "He [God] has favored our undertakings." The founding fathers credited Providence for siding with them in establishing a new nation.

The Roman numerals are the date of the Declaration of Independence and are the same as Roman numerals on the Statue of Liberty's tablet.

The words under the pyramid, Novus Ordo Seclorum, mean a new order for the ages to represent the American era.

Money, money, money! People carry money with them in their pockets and purses. On each piece of money are at least two symbols. An outline or silhouette of an important person in American history is on the front side. The backside of coins and bills are more diverse. Some have buildings, some have symbols, and some have events. The images on coins and bills can be changed. What do you recognize on these coins and bills?

From 1999 through 2008, the U.S. Mint produced the most popular series of coins: **The 50 State Quarters Program.**

How people treat their nation's symbols shows others how much they love their country. In the United States, respect for the flag is shown in different ways. The flag flies during the day, from sunrise to sunset. When the flag is raised or lowered, it should never touch the ground. When the flag is taken down, it is folded in a certain way. Flags fly at all government buildings including courthouses, post offices, and schools. When someone important dies, the flag flies at half-mast to honor them.

Have you noticed how people show respect when the National Anthem is sung or played? Many Americans show respect for their country and its symbols by standing, being quiet, putting their hand over their hearts, and taking their hats off.

However, each American is a symbol with individual concepts of equality, respect, and patriotism. Some Americans may kneel and bow their heads when the National Anthem is played. How we behave and show respect for our country's symbols is important; the constitution gives Americans the right of free speech.

Symbols tell others how important a country is to the people who live there. Many people wear American symbols on their clothing or buy things with American symbols on them to show others they identify with the United States of America.

Be on the lookout for American symbols. You will see them everywhere!

ABOUT THE AUTHOR:

Pat Daniel Jones grew up in a U.S. Air Force family. She lived in Louisiana, Guam, and Michigan as a child. As an adult, she has lived in Texas, Oklahoma, Kentucky, and Florida. She loves traveling and has visited the U.S. Capitol, Washington, D.C., numerous times. Her brother's family and her daughter's family lived just outside Washington, D.C. giving her multiple opportunities for visits!

https://bestmapsever.com/pages/us-national-monuments-list

https://www.nps.gov

https://www.nps.gov/stli

https://passionpassport.com/20-best-us-national-monuments

https://www.uscurrency.gov/denominations

https://www.usmint.gov/learn/coin-and-medal-programs/circulating-coins

www.ingramcontent.com/pod-product-compliance
Lightning Source LLC
Chambersburg PA
CBHW042002070526
44584CB00005BA/319